PERFECT PETS

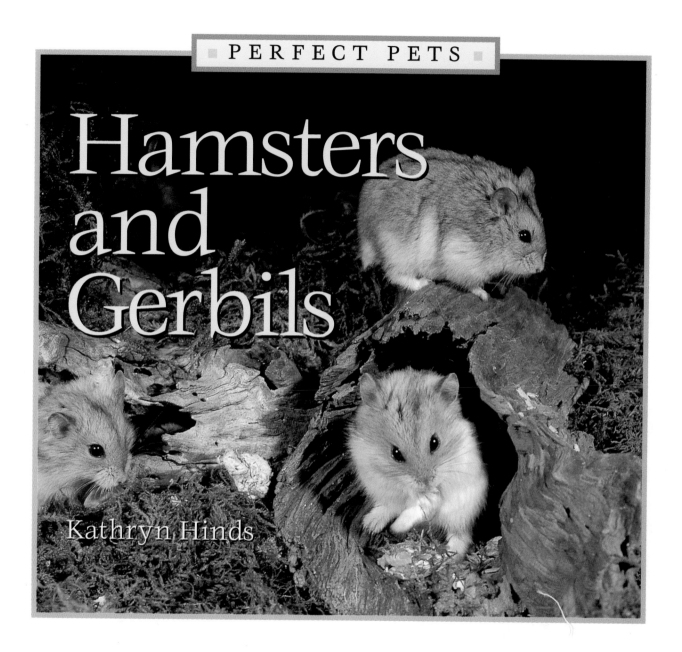

Hamsters and Gerbils

Kathryn Hinds

BENCHMARK BOOKS

MARSHALL CAVENDISH

NEW YORK

Benchmark Books
Marshall Cavendish Corporation
99 White Plains Road
Tarrytown, New York 10591

Library of Congress Cataloging-in-Publication Data
Hinds, Kathryn, date.
Hamsters and Gerbils/by Kathryn Hinds.
p.   cm. — (Perfect Pets)
Includes bibliographical references (p.) and index.
Summary: Describes the characteristics, habits, habitat, and history of gerbils and hamsters and how to raise them as pets.
ISBN 0-7614-1104-6 (lb)
1. Hamsters as pets—Juvenile literature.   2. Gerbils as pets—Juvenile literature [1. Hamsters as pets.   2. Gerbils   3. Pets.]
I. Title. II. Series.
SF459.H3 H56   2001   636.'356 dc21   99-058089   CIP   AC

Photo research by Candlepants, Inc.

Front and back cover photo: *Animals Animals*: Robert Maier

The photographs in this book are used by permission and through the courtesy of: *Animals Animals*: Zig Leszczynski, title, 10; Robert Maier, 3, 4, 16, 19, 22, 23, 29; Breck P. Kent, 17; Augustin J. Stevens, 18; J & P Wegner, 20; Michael Habicht, 24; *Art Resource*: Scala, 6. *Corbis/Bettmann*: Charles E. Rotkin, 7; Michael Maslan Historic Photographs, 11. *Photofest*: 8. *Photo Researchers, Inc.*: H. Rienhard/OKAPIA, 12; Carolyn A. McKeone, 13, 21, 25, 28, 30; Lemoine/JACANA, 14; Jerome Wexler, 15, 26, 27.

Printed in China
6   5

To my editor, Peter Mavrikis—
thanks for giving me such fun books to write!

A mother Syrian hamster and her babies help themselves to some ripening grain.

Hamsters

and gerbils are beloved pets in many parts of the world today. But not long ago, farmers simply thought of them as pests that stole grain from their fields. Both creatures were also well-known for **hoarding** food. During times of hunger, Chinese peasants would dig up hamster nests to get the grain the little animals had stored.

In Turkey and some Middle Eastern countries, gray hamsters have long been known as "house-haunting" hamsters. Like house mice, they make their nests in the walls of people's homes. The hamsters are fussier than mice, though—mice don't mind living in old houses, but gray hamsters only seem to like clean, new homes!

No one thought of keeping hamsters or gerbils as pets until the 20th century. In the 1930s, scientists began to study both animals in laboratories. This was the first time that hamsters and gerbils were raised in captivity. Pet shops began to sell hamsters in 1945, but it took another twenty years for people to realize that gerbils made good pets, too.

Now, millions of people in North American, Europe, Japan, Australia, and elsewhere enjoy the companionship of these lively little animals.

An Italian artist made this painting of a jerboa before the year 1632. The word gerbil comes from a word meaning "little jerboa." Gerbils have many similarities to jerboas, but they actually belong to a different animal family.

How Hamsters Became Pets

In 1930 Saul Adler, a doctor in Jerusalem, was doing research on cures for tropical diseases. He needed a particular kind of animal to test these cures. His friend, Israel Aharoni, was visiting the nearby country of Syria and knew of some creatures there that might be just right for Dr. Adler. These mouselike animals, golden hamsters, lived in only one part of Syria. Professor Aharoni asked villagers in the area to help him find a few of them. After digging in a wheat field for some time, a group of men finally found a mother hamster and eleven babies curled up in their nest.

Professor Aharoni and his wife took ten baby hamsters home with them. Mrs. Aharoni was charmed by the lively, golden-furred animals. She stayed up late at night feeding and looking after them. But one night while she was sleeping, the hamsters escaped from their cage. Eventually, the Aharonis caught all but one of the runaway rodents. Soon afterward, the professor took the hamsters to a laboratory at the university where he and Dr. Adler worked. A couple months later, one of the female hamsters had babies. These babies were given to Dr. Adler. When they had babies of their own, he gave some of them to scientists in France, England, Egypt, and India.

A scientist working with a hamster.

All these researchers found that hamsters were friendly and easy to handle. Some of the scientists gave hamsters to their children, and the little rodents turned out to be very good pets. It wasn't long before pet shops realized this, too. By 1950, hamsters were popular pets throughout Europe and North America.

8 *Pinky and the Brain work on one of Brain's plans to take over the world. Fortunately for Brain, Snowball the hamster is not around at the moment.*

Horrific Hamsters

Pet hamsters are so small and cute, it's difficult to imagine them doing any harm. And, except for chewing on things, they usually don't. But creators of books, comic books, TV shows, and games have had fun imagining hamsters whose bad behavior goes way beyond naughtiness.

R.L. Stine's Goosebumps book *Monster Blood II* features Cuddles the hamster, who eats some green slime called Monster Blood. The strange substance makes Cuddles grow to the size of an elephant and gives him a mean temper, too. He chews up everything in sight and terrorizes a boy and his family.

A mean but funny hamster appears in *Pinky and the Brain* comics and TV programs from time to time. His name is Snowball, and he is competing with Brain, a superintelligent mouse, to take over the world.

In the video game *Toe Jam* and *Earl*, the "bad guys" are hamsters. They roll around inside their hamster balls and squish anything that doesn't get out of their way in time.

A nicer hamster appears in the computer game *Day of the Tentacle*. This hamster helps the hero by running around in a wheel that is hooked up to a generator and produces electricity.

Pet hamsters today have a variety of different fur colors—even peach, like the fur of this young teddy bear hamster. The little rodent looks very content among the flowers!

Hamsters

and gerbils are **rodents**, like mice, guinea pigs, squirrels, and beavers. All rodents have large front teeth on top and bottom. These teeth are like sharp chisels that never stop growing. They are ideal for gnawing on things, which makes rodents good at chewing through wood and similar materials.

Different kinds of wild hamsters live from Eastern Europe all the way to China. Wild gerbils have an even larger range. There are about ninety **species**, or types, living throughout Africa, the Middle East, and Central Asia. For the most part, both animals live in dry **habitats** such as grasslands and deserts. They escape

A picture of a Syrian hamster in an old French dictionary of natural history. When this dictionary was written, very little was known about Syrian hamsters. (The animal above the hamster is a giant Malabar squirrel from India.)

11

It is easy to see why the Syrian hamster is also known as the golden hamster. Its fur can come in many shades of gold, from yellowish gold to dark reddish gold.

Some male teddy bear hamsters have long, thick fur all over their bodies, and some have long tufts of fur just at their hips. Others, like this one, look like they are wearing long fur skirts!

from extremes of heat and cold by burrowing deep into the ground. This also helps keep them safe from snakes, foxes, owls, and other **predators**.

The most common kind of pet hamster is the Syrian, or golden, hamster. It is bigger than a mouse but smaller than a rat, and it has hardly any tail. Golden hamsters originally came from the countryside around Aleppo, a city in the Middle Eastern nation of Syria. This is the only place where these hamsters have ever been found in the wild.

The original Syrian hamster had short, smooth, golden brown or reddish gold fur. Now, there are several other varieties of Syrian hamster. One of the favorites is the teddy bear (or long-haired) hamster. Male teddy bear hamsters have longer, thicker fur than females. Rex hamsters have wavy fur-even their whiskers are curled. Satin hamsters have extremely shiny fur. In the United States, some pet shops and hamster breeders offer hairless hamsters.

Syrian hamsters today sport many colors in addition to the original golden hue. Among them are cinnamon, rust, copper, blond, honey, yellow, white, cream, various shades of gray, and black. These colors can be combined in different patterns, too. Tortoiseshell hamsters are golden, gray, black, and cinnamon with yellow splotches. Banded hamsters have white bellies and a band of white around their middles; the rest of their fur can be any other color. Dominant-spot hamsters are white with colored spots or blotches on their backs

A white and cream banded Syrian hamster.

and heads. Roan hamsters are white with colored hairs scattered throughout their fur. White-bellied hamsters can be any color, but their stomachs are always pure white.

There are only a couple of other species of hamster that are commonly kept as pets. Dwarf Russian hamsters are smaller than Syrian hamsters. They have furry feet, so they are sometimes called hairy-footed hamsters. There are two kinds of dwarf Russian hamsters. The more often seen one is the dwarf Cambell's hamster. Its close relative is the Siberian (or winter white) hamster. Dwarf Cambells' have almost as many shades and types of fur as Syrian hamsters. Siberian hamsters are usually dark gray, but they sometimes turn white in the winter.

The Chinese hamster is one of the many kinds of gray hamsters that are found from Greece

A white and brown banded Syrian hamster.

15

There are eighty-seven different species of gerbils. This is an Egyptian gerbil, or desert mouse. It is sometimes kept as a pet.

to China. They are popular pets in China, where people even hold little circuses with trained hamsters doing tricks. Chinese hamsters have only two colors, their natural grayish-brown and white with grayish brown spots. They have the longest tails of any hamsters.

Although there are more species of gerbils than of hamsters, most pet gerbils are Mongolian gerbils. They are natives of Central Asia. Forty of the little rodents were captured in 1935, and they became the ancestors of all pet Mongolian gerbils.

Mongolian gerbils are smaller than hamsters but a bit bigger than mice. They have long, furry tails, often with a little tuft on the end. Their original color is a grayish brown. Today's pet gerbils exist in a wide range of other colors, too. In addition to black, white, cream, golden, honey, brown, and gray, there are colors such as red fox (bright reddish orange), blue fox (silvery gray), blue (dark bluish gray), and sapphire (light bluish gray). Some of these colors may combine in spotted patterns. Other combinations are also possible. The dark-tailed white, or Himalayan, is white with a brown tail. Colorpoints and Schimmels have a light color for most of their fur but are darker on the nose, ears, feet, and tail. This great variety of fur types and colors is one of the things that makes pet hamsters and gerbils so appealing to many animal lovers.

A Mongolian gerbil. Its grayish brown color helps it to blend in with its surroundings.

This mother and her babies are Setzer's hairy-footed gerbils. They live in Namibia in southwestern Africa.

One

of the most special things about gerbils and hamsters is that they are still basically wild animals. Even in a human home, they behave much like they would in their natural habitat. If gerbils are given a little sandbox, they will roll in it to give themselves "sand baths." A hamster will stuff its cheek pouches full of food, then hide the food under the bedding in its cage. These are just a couple of the wild behaviors that people with gerbils and hamsters are able to see. Watching and playing with these little rodents is also a way to experience a bit of the far-off lands that hamsters and gerbils came from.

There are a couple of very important differences between hamsters and gerbils. First, Syrian hamsters are **solitary** animals. This means that they must live alone. Syrian hamsters

A Syrian hamster stuffs its cheek pouches with seeds.

19

For this Siberian hamster on the loose, a drawer is a fun place to play hide-and-seek!

cannot share a cage without fighting each other. Chinese and Russian dwarf hamsters can live in pairs or groups, though, if they begin doing so at a young age. Gerbils live in large groups in the wild, so it's unkind to keep only one gerbil as a pet. It will be lonely and miserable without at least one companion. Gerbils like to play games with each other. They also spend a lot of time cleaning each other, and they often sleep curled up together.

The second major difference has to do with when these rodents are active. Hamsters are **nocturnal**, which means they stay awake all night and sleep all day. Gerbils sleep off and on throughout the day and night. In between naps they eat and play, no matter what time it is. One other difference is that gerbils have a lifespan of four to five years, while hamsters usually live for two to three years.

Both animals are very quiet. They will squeak if they are

Gerbils Can Jump!

Gerbils have very powerful hind legs. They use them to kick dirt out of the way when they are digging their **burrows**. These strong rear legs also make gerbils great jumpers. In the wild, they can quickly jump away from predators. Young pet gerbils often seem to jump just for joy. Older gerbils will jump to reach food placed up high or to get out of a small enclosure. They can jump more than a foot straight up into the air—so be careful where you put them while you are cleaning out their cage!

This mother is ready to protect her babies, who are about twenty days old.

21

A pet Egyptian gerbil stands up on its hind legs for a good look around.

scared, and gerbils thump their back feet on the ground when they are startled. Usually, though, hamsters and gerbils communicate by body language. A hamster that is curious about something may lift one of its front paws off the ground. A frightened hamster may tilt its head to one side and draw its paws close to its body. Gerbils have been known to wink when they are feeling happy. Both hamsters and gerbils stand up on their hind legs when they want to get a good look around. They also sniff the air or along the ground to track the scents of friends, enemies, and food.

Hamsters and gerbils are extremely clean. They do not smell bad, and they never need to be bathed. Gerbils groom each other, and Syrian hamsters wash themselves in the same way that cats do. Teddy bear hamsters, however, have to be brushed often, or their long fur will become tangled.

Since hamsters and gerbils are small animals, they don't need much room. Unlike cats, they do not need a

This Siberian hamster can have a lot of fun going in and out of its little house and crawling through a tube.

litter box. Unlike dogs, they do not need to be walked. Because they are so easy to care for, so clean, and so quiet, they make very good pets for busy families and for people who live in apartments.

A little house like this is a nice thing to add to a hamster's or gerbil's cage. It gives the animal a cozy, private place to curl up for a nap. And there's a great view from the window!

One

special thing that hamsters and gerbils do need is the right kind of home. A large aquarium is the best home for gerbils and dwarf hamsters, who are very good at squeezing between cage bars. There should be screening over the top of the aquarium to let in plenty of air. This top needs to be securely fastened so that the little animals do not escape.

Dwarf hamsters can live in a plastic hamster home that has tunnels leading from one section to another. These are sold in many stores and can be very colorful and fun. They are not always the best homes for Syrian hamsters, who can get too big to go through the tunnels. (And gerbils will chew right through the plastic of these homes.) A Syrian hamster can be quite happy in a cage or a large aquarium.

The floor of the hamster's or gerbil's home needs to be

Gerbils like to live together in groups. They also like to run around and explore, so if you put them in a cage, make sure they won't be able to squeeze out between the bars. It will also help to give them a large cage with lots to do inside it.

covered with some kind of bedding. Aspen shavings, crushed corncobs, and chopped straw or hay (make sure it's not moldy, though) are the best materials. Cedar and pine shavings are the worst—they can be poisonous to these little animals. Peat and clean play sand are other possibilities. These can be messy, but on the other hand, they are great for the rodents to dig in and tunnel.

The cage or aquarium must be kept out of direct sunlight and away from drafts. It will get too hot if it is near a radiator or heater. Gerbils and hamsters also prefer to be in a fairly calm and quiet area—not right next to the TV, for example. And, of course, the little rodents must not be placed anywhere that a cat or dog can get to them!

If you need to weigh your hamster, here's one way to do it!

Hamsters and gerbils will choose one corner of their home to use as a bathroom. This area should be cleaned every day. The rest of the enclosure needs to be cleaned only when it gets smelly or looks very dirty. This could be once a week or even once a month.

A hanging water bottle ought to be placed in the cage or aquarium. It should always be clean and full. A sturdy food bowl is another must. Wild gerbils and hamsters eat seeds,

A carrot slice is just the right size for a hamster to nibble.

grains, grasses, and small insects. Pets should be given a balanced gerbil or hamster food, which you can buy at the store. They can also have small amounts of fresh vegetables. Alfalfa, broccoli, celery, carrots, peas, dandelion leaves, and clover are all safe and nutritious foods for these animals. And they love to get sunflower seeds and peanuts as treats.

Offering treats is a good way to begin taming a new hamster or gerbil. These animals are very shy and nervous at first. But they are curious, too. So slowly reach your hand into their home and give them a chance to smell you a couple times a day before you start handling them. Talk to them quietly and gently so that they get used to your voice, too. Soon, they will probably start climbing onto your hand.

After three or four days, you can try to pick up your hamster or gerbil. Because these are small animals, they need careful handling. The Syrian hamster is the easiest of these rodents to handle and the easiest to tame. Gerbils will almost always run away when you want to pick them up. This is simply their **instinct**. Be patient and calm. If you keep your hand still inside their home, they should settle down. Then you can gently scoop up a gerbil in your cupped hands. Always pick up hamsters and gerbils from underneath. A hand coming down from above is very

It is very important to hold hamsters and gerbils carefully and gently. This four-year-old boy has learned to handle his pet hamster in just the right way.

scary to them. It will also frighten them if you try to pick them up while they are sleeping. Once you are holding your pet, sit down on the floor. This way, if it wriggles out of your hands, it is not in danger of falling.

After about two weeks, you will be able to play with your hamster or gerbil. Let it walk around on you and maybe climb onto your shoulder. Sometimes hamsters and gerbils will learn to enjoy riding around in your shirt pocket. (It helps if you put a raisin or sunflower seed in your pocket first!) They can also travel around parts of the house (away from stairs and other dangers) inside an exercise ball. This is a plastic ball, with air holes, that the animal can run inside of. As it runs, the ball rolls around.

Of course, hamsters and gerbils enjoy playing inside their homes as well. Both animals like to run on little wheels. The safest wheels have solid bottoms. Ladders and things to crawl in and out of are fun, too. Some hamsters and gerbils even like to walk on a tightrope!

Gerbils and hamsters are fun to watch. They are cute, lively, and acrobatic. They are fun to hold and pet, too. The more you handle and play with your pet—so long as you are gentle—the tamer it will be. There is no feeling quite like the happiness of making friends with an animal!

Hamsters and gerbils love to run on wheels, and it's great exercise for them. Most hamsters are safe on wheels like this one, but gerbils and dwarf hamsters are safest on wheels with solid bottoms.

Fun Facts

ᘺ Gerbils mate for life.

ᘺ The gerbil's scientific name, *Meriones unguiculatus*, means "little clawed warrior."

ᘺ Hamsters got their name from the German word *hamstern*, which means "to hoard, or store up."

ᘺ The common (or European) hamster has been known to store as much as one-hundred pounds (forty-five kilograms) of food in its burrow.

ᘺ Gerbils are sometimes called sand rats or desert rats.

ᘺ A mother gerbil can give birth to ten babies at a time.

ᘺ A mother hamster can give birth to twenty-four babies at a time (but eight or ten is more usual).

ᘺ Syrian hamsters were brought to the United States for the first time in the summer of 1938.

ᘺ Gerbils lived in captivity for the first time in Japan in the 1930s. They came to the United States in 1954.

Glossary

burrow: To dig a hole in the ground for an animal to live in; also, the hole or nest dug out by an animal (such as a gerbil).

hoard: To store up and hide large amounts of something.

habitat: The area in which an animal normally lives.

instinct: A type of response that an animal is born with.

nocturnal: Awake and active during the night.

predator: An animal that hunts other animals for food.

rodents: Animals that have large, constantly growing front teeth that they use for gnawing.

solitary: Used to living alone.

species: A group of animals that are descended from the same ancestor and are alike in certain ways.

Find Out More About Hamsters and Gerbils

Evans, Mark. *Hamster*. New York: Dorling Kindersley, 1993.

Fox, Dr. Michael. *Hamsters and Rabbits*. New York: Tulchin Studios and Maier Communications, 1989. (videotape)

Harper, Don. *Hamsters and Gerbils*. New York: Smithmark, 1996.

Hearne, Tina. *Gerbils*. Vero Beach, Florida: Rourke Publications, 1989.

Pope, Joyce. *Taking Care of Your Gerbils*. London, New York, and Toronto: Franklin Watts, 1987.

You can also get information from a number of Web sites, including:

Caring for Hamsters, http://www.hamstercare.co.uk/

Mongolian Gerbils, http://www.rodentfancy.com/pets/gerbils/

The Internet is always changing, and you may need to ask your library's media specialist to help you find the information.

Index

About the Author

Kathryn Hinds grew up near Rochester, New York, and always wanted to be a writer. She has been an animal lover ever since she was given her first pet, a kitten, when she was three years old. Kathryn now lives in Georgia's Blue Ridge Mountains with her husband, their son, three cats, and three dogs. Her other *Perfect Pets* books are *Cats* and *Rabbits*. She has also written several books in Marshall Cavendish's *Cultures of the Past* series and four books about *Life in the Middle Ages*. In her spare time, Kathryn likes to dance, read, listen to music, and take long walks in the woods.